ANIMALS ARE AMAZING
DOLPHINS

BY KATE RIGGS

W
FRANKLIN WATTS
LONDON • SYDNEY

This edition published in the UK in 2014 by
Franklin Watts
338 Euston Road
London NW1 3BH

Franklin Watts Australia
Level 17/207 Kent Street
Sydney NSW 2000

First published by Creative Education,
an imprint of the Creative Company
Copyright © 2012 Creative Education
International copyright reserved in all countries.

ISBN 978 1 4451 2960 0
Dewey number: 599.5'3

A CIP catalogue record for this book is
available from the British Library.

Printed in China

Franklin Watts is a division of Hachette Children's
Books, an Hachette UK company
www.hachette.co.uk

Design and production by The Design Lab
Art direction by Rita Marshall

Photographs by Dreamstime (Pwozza, Skynesher,
Stephenmeese), Getty Images (Georgette Douwma,
Mustafa Ozer/AFP, Flip Nicklin, Gail Shumway,
Stuart Westmorland, Norbert Wu), and iStockphoto
(Lars Christensen, Jose Manuel Gelpi Diaz, Nancy
Nehring, Tammy Peluso, James Steidl)

CONTENTS

What are dolphins?

Dolphins are animals that live in the oceans. Scientists think that dolphins may be one of the cleverest animals in the world. There are more than 30 kinds of dolphins in the wild. Bottlenose dolphins, spinner dolphins and common dolphins are three of the most popular types.

A bottlenose dolphin looks like it is smiling because of the shape of its mouth.

oceans big areas of deep, salty water.

Dolphin facts

Dolphins have smooth skin and lots of small teeth.

Most dolphins have smooth grey skin, which feels a bit like rubber. A flat tail and fins help them to swim through the water. Their noses are called beaks because they are a long, thin shape. Dolphins have lots of small teeth – some dolphins have more than 200! They breathe air through a blowhole on top of their heads.

blowhole a hole in the top of a dolphin's head that opens when the dolphin breathes in.

Big and small dolphins

The smallest dolphins, such as the Hector's dolphin, weigh less than 45 kilogrammes. Dolphins like the bottlenose dolphin are much bigger. Male bottlenose dolphins can weigh more than 450 kilogrammes! Female dolphins are usually smaller than the males. Bigger types of dolphin usually live in deeper water than smaller dolphins.

Dolphins of all sizes like to play with seaweed!

Where dolphins live

*People often see dolphins
swimming close to the shore.*

All dolphins live in water. Some live in salty seawater and some live in rivers, too. Dolphins don't like very cold water, so many dolphins live near the equator (*ee-KWAY-ter*), where it is always warm.

equator the area around the middle part of the Earth where the weather is the warmest.

Dolphin food

Dolphins eat food from the ocean. Some of their favourite foods to eat are small fish such as mackerel. Sometimes dolphins eat squid and crabs, too. Dolphins don't chew their food, they swallow it whole.

This dolphin has caught a fish to eat.

New dolphins

A mother dolphin has one calf at a time. The calf stays close to its mother to stay safe. Dolphins are mammals and calfs drink their mother's milk for about 18 months. They start eating fish when their teeth come through. At about two years old they start learning how to hunt. Calves stay with their mother until they are between three and six years old. Most wild dolphins can live for about 25 years.

Dolphin calves swim close to their mother to stay safe.

calf a baby dolphin.
mammal animals that drink milk from their mother when they are a baby.

Life in a pod

Dolphins live in groups called **pods**. Small pods have up to 15 dolphins. **Super-pods** can have hundreds of dolphins in them. Dolphins spend a lot of their time swimming and playing. Dolphins can swim fast – up to 35 kilometres an hour. That's as fast as a car!

Dolphins like to leap, dive and swim together.

pod a group of dolphins.
super-pod when lots of smaller pods join together, often when dolphins want to hunt large shoals of fish.

Hunting for food

Dolphins work together to hunt for food. They 'talk' to each other using clicking and whistling sounds. If one dolphin spots a group of fish to eat, it tells the other dolphins. Dolphins dive down to find their food, too. Some dolphins can dive down more than 300 metres, but most dives are much less than this. Dolphins can hold their breath under water for up to 12 minutes.

A big dolphin pod can catch and eat many fish.

Dolphins and people

Today, some people go on boats to see dolphins in the wild. Sometimes they swim with them. Other people visit **aquariums** (*ah-KWARE-ee-ums*) to see dolphins. It is exciting to see these clever animals jump out of the water!

Dolphins like to jump high out of the water when they play.

aquarium buildings where fish and other water animals are kept in big, glass tanks.

A *dolphin story*

There are many stories of dolphins helping humans. This is one from Greece. Once, a famous singer named Arion was sailing on a boat. He had a lot of money because he had won a competition. There were bad men on the boat who wanted to hurt Arion and steal his money. So he jumped overboard. A dolphin saw him and carried him on its back to the shore. Arion was safe! From then on, dolphins and humans were friends.

Useful information

Read More

If You Were A: Dolphin by Clare Hibbert (Franklin Watts, 2013)

Watery Worlds: The Open Ocean by Jinny Johnson
(Franklin Watts, 2011)

Animal Instincts: A Curious Dolphin by Tom Jackson (Wayland, 2013)

Saving Wildlife: Ocean Wildlife by Sonya Newland
(Franklin Watts, 2014)

Websites

*http://kids.nationalgeographic.co.uk/kids/animals/creaturefeature/
bottlenose-dolphin/*
This site has lots of facts and photos of the bottlenose dolphin.

http://www.dolphins.org/kids_area.php
The Dolphin Research Centre has a "Kids Area" with fun activities.

Every effort has been made by the Publishers to ensure that these websites are suitable for
children, that they are of the highest educational value and that they contain no inappropriate
or offensive material. However, because of the nature of the Internet, it is impossible to guarantee
that the contents of these sites will not be altered. We strongly advise that Internet access is
supervised by a responsible adult.

Index